MEL BAY'S
EASIEST
ACCORDION
BOOK

BY NEIL GRIFFIN

1 2 3 4 5 6 7 8 9 0

Visit us on the Web at http://www.melbay.com — E-mail us at email@melbay.com

CONTENTS

ABOUT THE LEFT HAND

The left hand of the accordion provides the "Bass and Chord" part of the music.

For purposes of this simple solo book we will only use 6 bass notes and 6 major chords, which is what a beginners style accordion has. This is called a "12-Bass accordion" and these 12 buttons are aligned exactly the same no matter which of the various size accordions own. Most accordions have 12, 24, 48, 80, or 120 bass buttons. Starting with the 12-Bass model each simply expands the number of notes, chords, and range of the previous model.

All solos in this book can be played on any of the above described intruments.

Shown below is the left hand fingering and the layout of the bass buttons......

This brief explanation is a review for new students as well as for Piano Students who wish to try some simple songs on the accordion...... HAVE FUN!!!

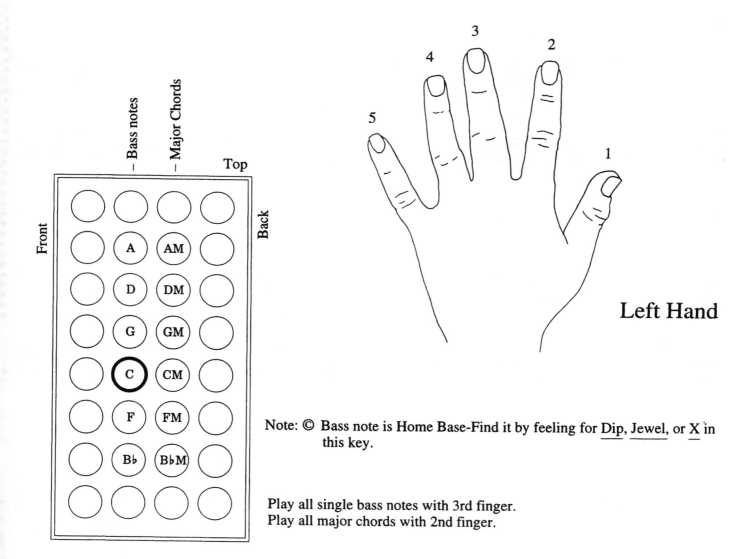

Note: © Bass note is Home Base-Find it by feeling for <u>Dip</u>, <u>Jewel</u>, or <u>X</u> in this key.

Play all single bass notes with 3rd finger.
Play all major chords with 2nd finger.

GOING HOME
(Largo)

Key of C
No Sharps or Flats

BARCAROLLE
(Theme)

Key of G
Sharp F's

Offenbach

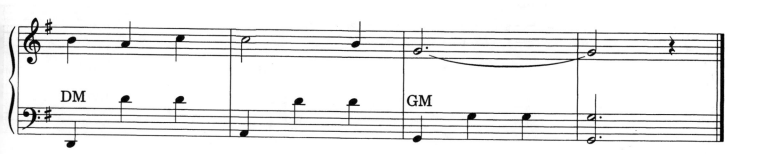

AMAZING GRACE

Key of G
Sharp F's

Organ Like

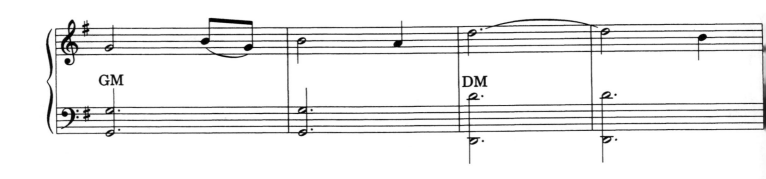

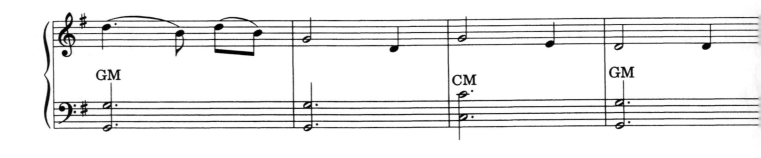

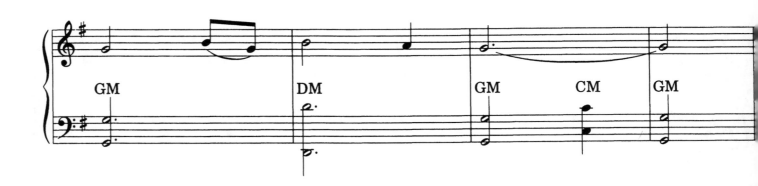

IRISH WASHERWOMAN

Key of G
Sharp F's

WHEN THE SAINTS GO MARCHING IN

Key of C
No Sharps or Flats

With Spirit

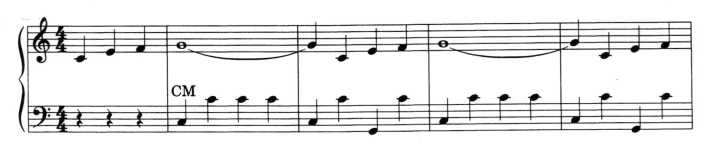

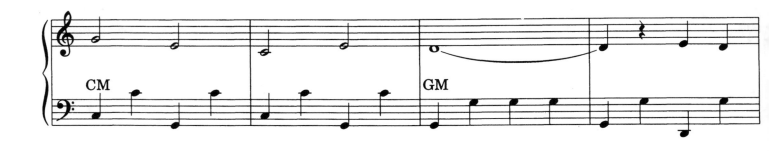

DOWN IN THE VALLEY

Key of G
Sharp F's

BEAUTIFUL BROWN EYES
(Medium Waltz)

Key of F
Flat B's

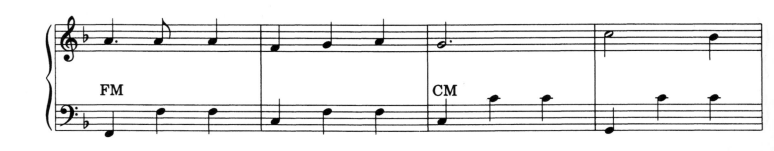

LAVENDER BLUE

Key of C
No Sharps or Flats

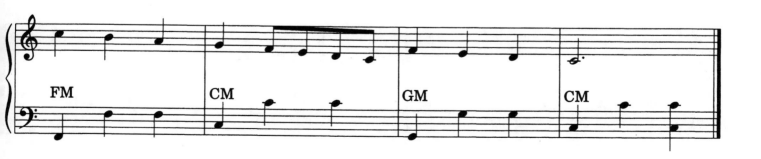

DU, DU LIEGST MIR IM HERZEN

Key of G
Sharp F's

ALOHA OE

Key of C
No Sharps or Flats

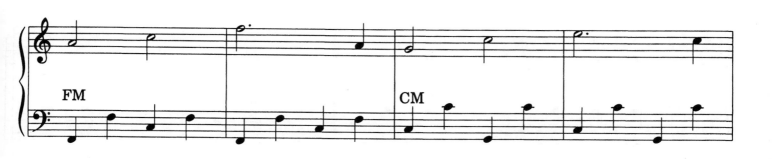

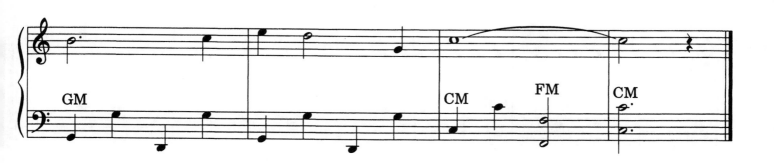

JINGLE BELLS

Key of C
No Sharps or Flats

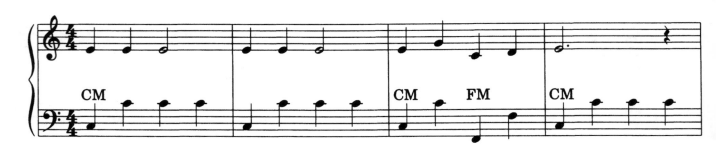

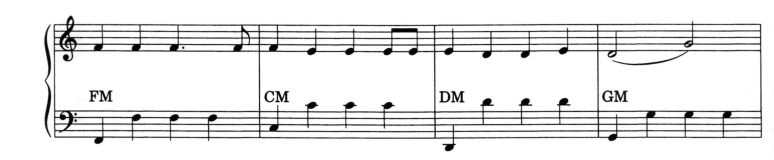

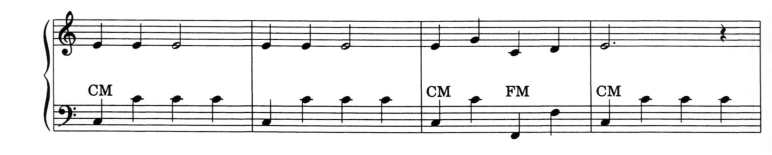

MARY ANN

Key of G
Sharp F's

Calypso

LOVE SOMEBODY

Key of D
Sharp F's and C's

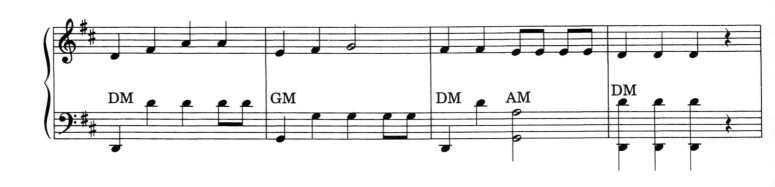

BLOW THE MAN DOWN

Key of C
No Sharps or Flats

Sea Chanty

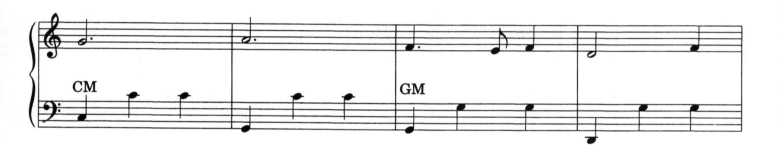

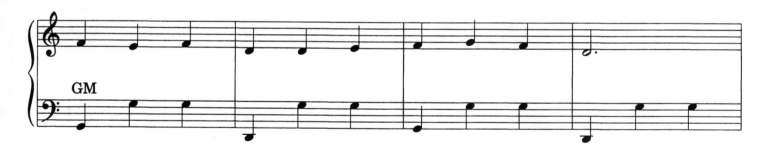

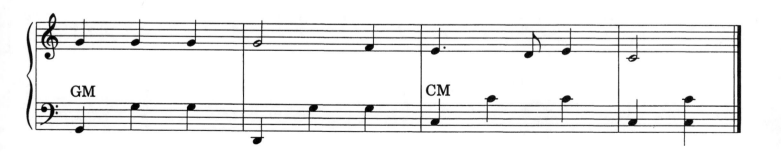

ALMA MATER

Key of C
No Sharps or Flats

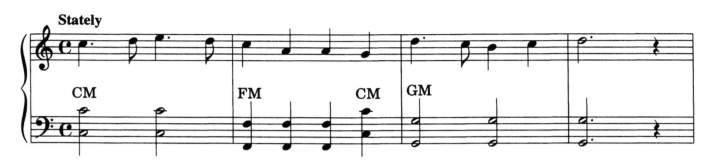

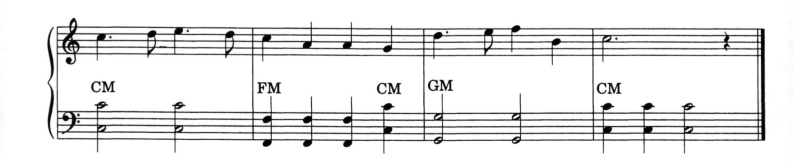

SONG FROM MAGIC FLUTE

Key of C
No Sharps or Flats

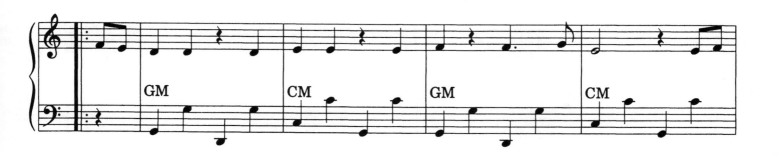

JUST A CLOSER WALK WITH THEE

Key of C
No Sharps or Flats

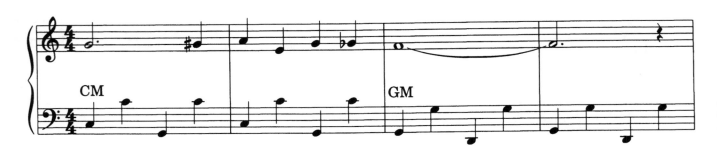

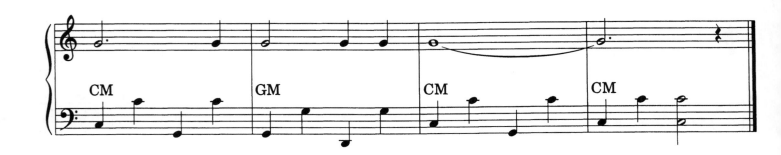

JUANITA

Key of F
Flat B's

FRANKIE AND JOHNNY

Key of D
Sharp F's and C's

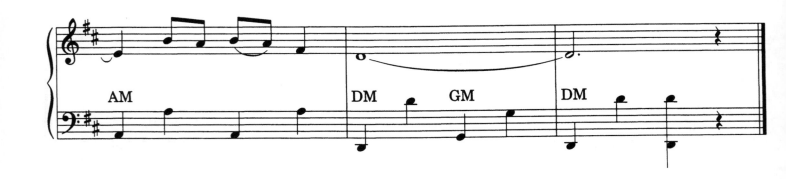

VIVE LA COMPAGNIE

Key of D
Sharp F's and C's

ALOUETTE

Key of G
Sharp F's

WHERE SHALL I BE?

Key of G
Sharp F's

Gospel

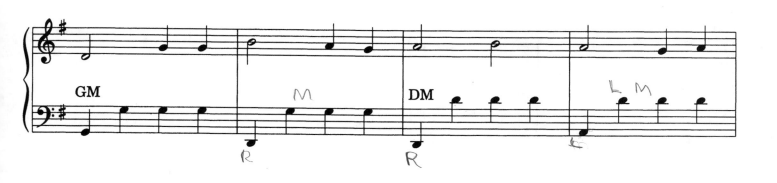

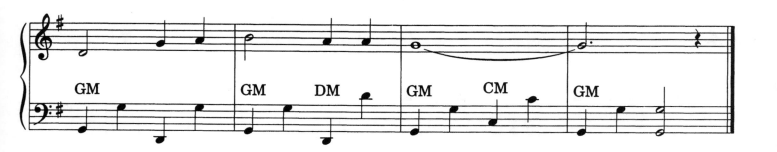

MY WILD IRISH ROSE

Key of C
No Sharps or Flats

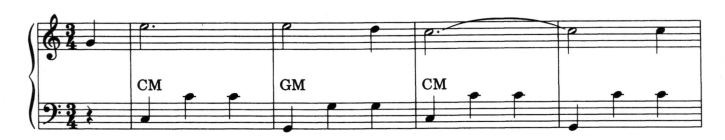

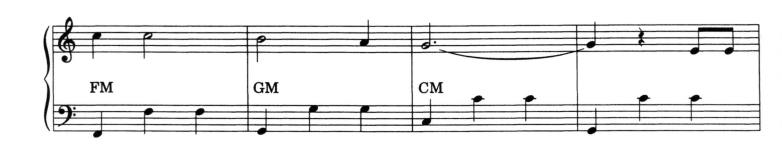

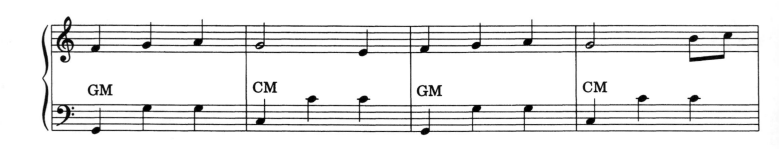

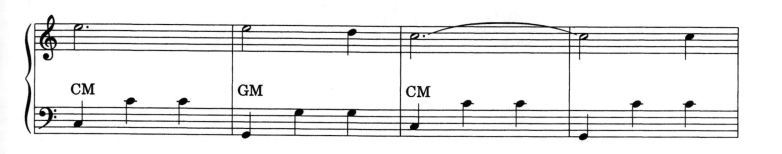

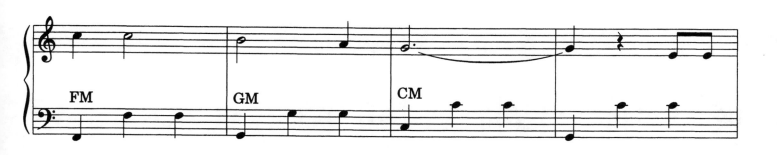

MOONLIGHT BAY

Key of G
Sharp F's

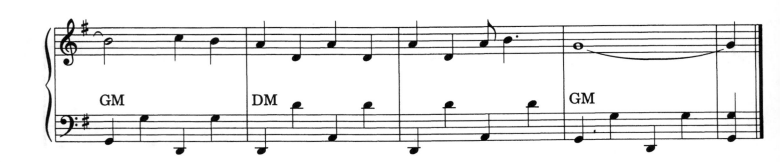

AWAY IN A MANGER

Key of G
Sharp F's

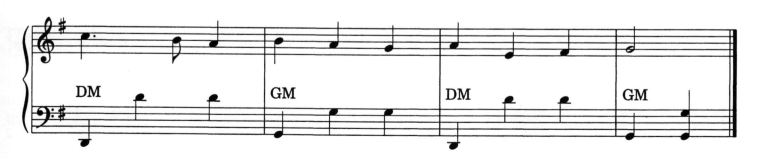

WHEN IRISH EYES ARE SMILING

Key of C
No Sharps or Flats

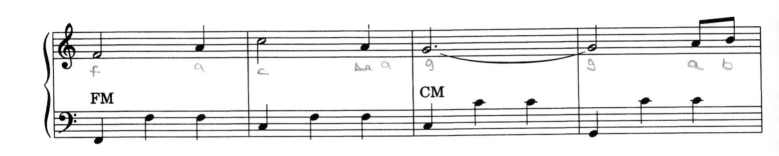

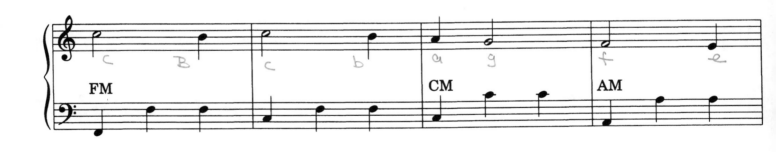

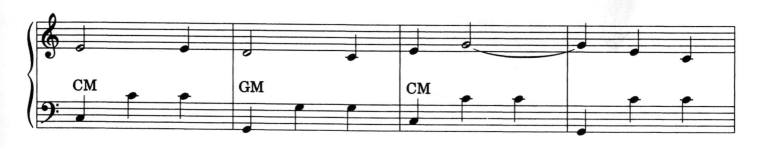

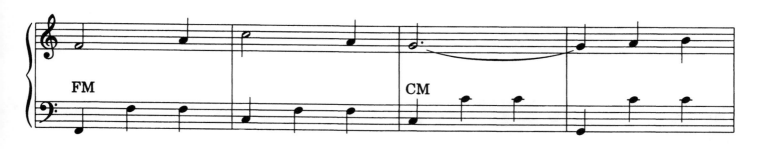

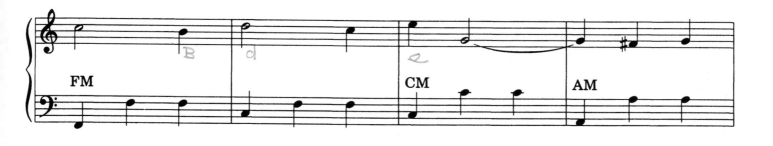

ALL THROUGH THE NIGHT

Key of G
Sharp F's